One Year Self-Discovery Journal for Black Women

365 Eye-Opening Questions to Discover Yourself, Raise Self Esteem, and Embrace Your True Beauty

Layla Moon

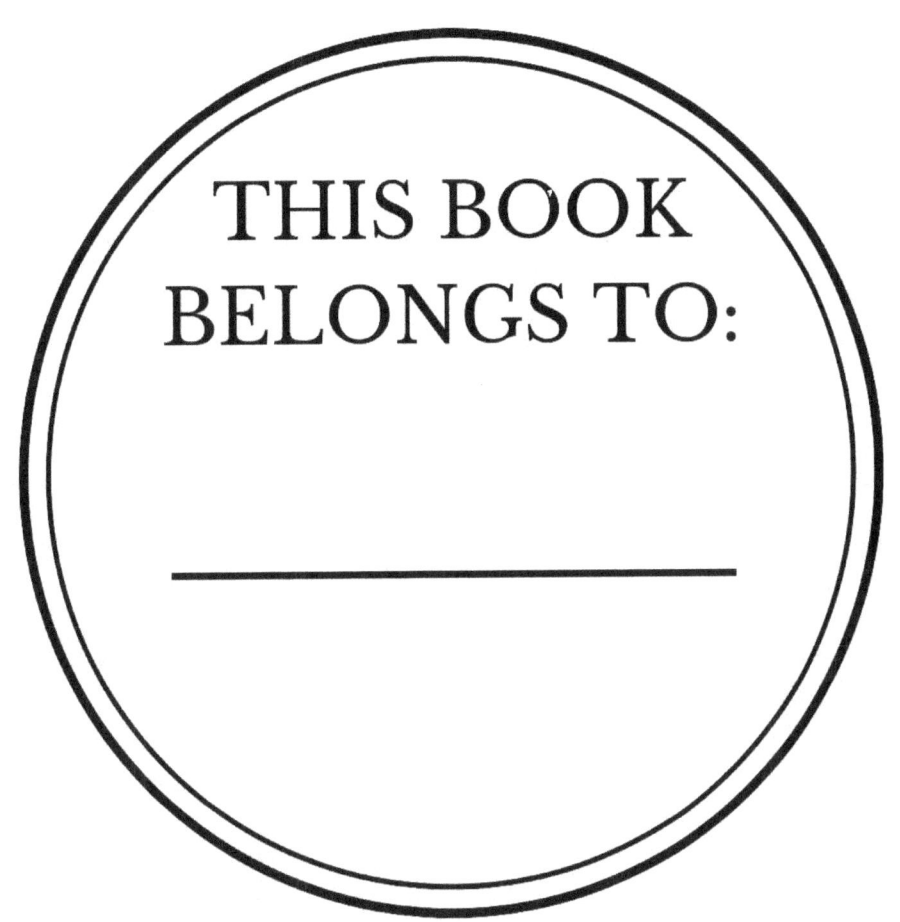

THIS BOOK
BELONGS TO:

_____

4 FREE Gifts

To help you along your spiritual journey, I've created 4 FREE bonus eBooks.

1. *Spirit Guides for Beginners: How to Hear the Universe's Call and Communicate with Your Spirit Guide and Guardian Angels*

2. **Law of Attraction: Manifest Your Desire**

3. *Hoodoo Book of Spells for Beginners: Easy and effective Rootwork, Conjuring, and Protection Spells for Healing and Prosperity*

4. **Book of Shadows**

You can get instant access by signing up to my email newsletter below.

On top of the 4 free books, you will also receive weekly tips along with free book giveaways, discounts, and so much more.

All of these bonuses are 100% free with no strings attached. You don't need to provide any personal information except your email address.

To get your bonus, go to:

https://dreamlifepress.com/four-free-gifts

Introduction

Asking questions is the best way to learn something. You do this on a daily basis without realizing it. It's the quickest method to receive the knowledge you need to get by, accomplish your goals, or understand your loved ones.

But what about your own self? Are you as interested in learning about yourself as you are in learning about others?

Self-reflection inquiries are similar to peeling an onion. New questions occur every time you believe you've discovered the solution. If you're intrigued by what's below, there's always another layer to remove.

Self-awareness is a lifelong process that is unique to each individual. The questions in this journal may or may not have definitive answers. However, they'll serve as a compass to guide you through your journey of self-discovery. You'll learn to accept who you are and love yourself unconditionally over the course of a year of daily self-reflection.

You cannot be self-aware or discover your true self without taking note of important questions and answers. Once you answer these questions, you should take it a step further by journaling.

Journaling is your best friend when it comes to solving important questions. You connect to your experiences differently when you write about them. When you put words on paper, your thinking shifts. Because handwriting is slower than typing, your mind is forced to slow down and pick words more carefully.

When you answer self-reflection questions in writing, you will get different results than when you answer them verbally. Don't filter what you write if you want to gain meaningful knowledge. Allow yourself to write without altering a single word in your journal.

This book contains some thought-provoking questions to help you become more self-aware. No one else will be able to answer these questions for you.

Remember: As a Black woman, you carry intrinsic power everywhere you go, and no one can take that away from you. So, remind yourself of this when you encounter difficult questions that require painful or intense self-reflection.

Day 1

As a black woman, the need to control everything is so deeply ingrained in us that surrendering is quite tough. We have been conditioned to believe that we must work things out on our own, yet this could not be farther from reality. Surrendering is recognizing that you have this amazing power (God, spirit, or the universe) at your side at all times to assist and support you.

"What do I need to surrender to the universe?"

_____

_____

_____

_____

_____

_____

_____

_____

_____

_____

_____

_____

_____

_____

_____

_____

_____

_____

_____

_____

_____

_____

_____

_____

Day 2

Sometimes it is okay to worry. We'd be more prone to make errors that might harm us, endanger our health, and wreck our future if we merely went through life aimlessly. However, "normal" worry can become troublesome if it persists and is difficult to manage.

So ask yourself:

"What do I need to stop worrying about? What can I do to stop worrying about these things?"

_____

_____

_____

_____

_____

_____

_____

_____

_____

_____

_____

_____

_____

_____

_____

_____

_____

_____

_____

_____

_____

_____

_____

_____

Day 3

"What stereotypes do people have about me?"

There are numerous stereotypes about black women, including that we are always angry, irritated, and loud. Write down two instances where you have been stereotyped and how this made you feel.

_____
_____
_____
_____
_____
_____
_____
_____
_____
_____
_____
_____
_____
_____
_____
_____
_____
_____
_____
_____
_____
_____
_____
_____
_____
_____

Day 4

"What three adjectives best characterize my personality?"

Knowing what describes your character could assist you in knowing if you need to further develop or consciously work on these traits. Doing this will help you become the best version of yourself.

_____

_____

_____

_____

_____

_____

_____

_____

_____

_____

Day 5

"What is the one thing that terrifies me the most right now? Why does it terrify me?"

Each time you learn something new and even go the extra mile in trying it out, you might be uncomfortable, but you are learning something. Putting yourself out there is not bad.

_____

_____

_____

_____

_____

_____

_____

_____

_____

Day 6

"What do I think about my current mental health?"

"What activities can I do to improve it?"

"How often should I undertake these activities?"

Experiencing racism and sexism as black women have messed with our mental health for decades. We are expected to be there for everyone. Despite the temptation to be a superhero, we are more likely to feel depressed, lonely, and nervous.

Some of us have been conditioned to believe that seeking mental health help is a taboo. Some Black women are unaware that their feelings are symptoms of anxiety or depression. This might make it difficult to determine whether or not assistance is required. The above questions will make you conscious of your mental health struggles and how to overcome them.

_____

_____

_____

_____

_____

_____

_____

_____

_____

_____

_____

_____

_____

_____

_____

_____

_____

_____

Day 7

"How do I rate my physical wellbeing?"

"What can I do to make my physical wellbeing better?"

Most times, with all the responsibilities we have, we forget to take care of our physical health. We have been conditioned to care for others and neglect ourselves. You cannot function optimally if your physical health is jeopardized. Take a moment to evaluate your physical health and find ways of improving it.

_____

_____

_____

_____

_____

_____

_____

_____

_____

_____

_____

_____

_____

_____

_____

_____

_____

_____

_____

_____

_____

_____

_____

_____

Day 8

"How can I handle my emotions properly?"

A cultural icon is a powerful Black lady. However, if we cling to that image instead of accepting and resolving the stress and trauma that so many have endured, our emotions will remain messed up. You need to examine how to handle your emotions in a healthier and more constructive manner.

_____

_____

_____

_____

_____

_____

_____

_____

_____

Day 9

"What about me makes me happy?"

Your happiness begins with you. Look inwardly and find out things about yourself that make you happy.

_____

_____

_____

_____

_____

_____

_____

_____

Day 10

"Which three characteristics about myself do I believe make me sad?"

If you do not love yourself, you will have self-esteem issues. If these characteristics can be worked on, then work on them.

_____

_____

_____

_____

_____

_____

_____

_____

_____

_____

_____

Day 11

"What is the most important thing to me right now?"

Answering this question helps you know what you should focus your energy on.

_____

_____

_____

_____

_____

_____

_____

_____

_____

_____

Day 12

"What would be one thing I'd want to do less of, and why?"

When you have an answer to this question, you will know what you need to let go of.

_____

_____

_____

_____

_____

_____

_____

_____

_____

_____

_____

Day 13

"What would be something I'd want to do more of, and why?"

Doing something you find pleasure in will help you physically, emotionally, and mentally.

_____

_____

_____

_____

_____

_____

_____

_____

_____

_____

Day 14

"When was the last time I helped someone else?"

One secret to happiness is helping someone.

There is a Chinese saying, "If you want happiness for an hour, take a nap. If you want happiness for a day, go fishing. If you want happiness for a year, inherit a fortune. If you want happiness for a lifetime, help somebody."

Helping others is the key to a richer, happier, healthier, more productive, and meaningful existence. What is important is that you don't hurt yourself while giving.

_____

_____

_____

_____

_____

_____

_____

_____

_____

_____

_____

_____

_____

_____

_____

_____

_____

_____

_____

_____

_____

Day 15

"What keeps me up in the middle of the night?"

Due to trauma you might have endured while growing up or the struggles of everyday living, there are things in your adult life that spark worry and keep you up at night. You need to figure out what keeps you up at night and deal with it.

_____

_____

_____

_____

_____

_____

_____

_____

_____

_____

_____

_____

_____

_____

_____

_____

_____

_____

_____

_____

_____

_____

_____

_____

_____

_____

_____

_____

Day 16

"Have I been stifling my creativity in any way?"

Everyone has a creative side. We can develop undesirable habits as we get older that act as mental barriers to our creativity. Like other bad habits, they can be broken if you are prepared to put in the effort.

You have to know how you have been jeopardizing your creativity. Answering this question puts you in a better position on your self-discovery path.

Day 17

"What are the roadblocks to my happiness?"

As a woman of color, you should know that no matter how hard you try, life will occasionally give you lemons. You might be at the point in your life where nothing seems to make you happy. This question will give you an insight into what is keeping you from being a happy black woman.

_____

_____

_____

_____

_____

_____

_____

_____

_____

_____

_____

_____

_____

_____

_____

_____

_____

_____

_____

_____

_____

_____

_____

_____

_____

_____

Day 18

"What are my most valuable assets?"

It does not have to be money or any material item. In fact, if your most valuable assets are material things, you will notice that you are never satisfied. You can also lose everything very fast.

Take time to answer this question. If your answer is a positive one, then you should focus on those assets.

_____

_____

_____

_____

_____

_____

_____

_____

_____

_____

_____

_____

_____

_____

_____

_____

_____

_____

_____

_____

_____

_____

_____

_____

Day 19

"What can I do to make myself happier?"

By now, you should know that you are the only one that can guarantee your happiness. As a black women, we have been conditioned to prioritize other people's happiness over ours. When you figure out what you can do to make yourself happy, as long as you are not hurting anyone, go for it!

_____

_____

_____

_____

_____

_____

_____

_____

_____

_____

Day 20

"What does it mean to me to be self-assured?"

When you are self-assured, you are self-confident. When you are confident, nothing can deter you.

_____

_____

_____

_____

_____

_____

_____

Day 21

"How can I turn a humbling situation into a good lesson and development opportunity?"

It is okay to fail at something. What is most important is that you learn from your mistakes. Black women are rarely given the opportunity to fail at something and try again. There may be snide and hurtful remarks. However, do not let that deter you. You need to remember that you've got your own back.

_____

_____

_____

_____

_____

_____

_____

_____

_____

_____

_____

_____

_____

_____

_____

_____

_____

_____

_____

_____

_____

_____

_____

_____

_____

Day 22

"What does personal and professional success mean to me?"

Success means different things to a lot of people. You need to figure out what it means to be successful. This will help you avoid the pitfalls of comparing yourself to other people.

_____

_____

_____

_____

_____

_____

_____

_____

_____

Day 23

"How frequently do I have doubts about my own abilities?"

Imposter syndrome is one of the unfortunate consequences of systemic oppression or conditioning that we are less-than or undeserving of achievement. By identifying how often you doubt your own abilities, you are in a better position to find ways of challenging these limiting beliefs and faulty conditioning.

_____

_____

_____

_____

_____

_____

_____

_____

Day 24

"Am I a leader or a follower?"

With all the ordeals we have had to face, it is possible to act as a follower even when you should be leading. This question lets you know which category you are in and if you should change.

_____
_____
_____
_____
_____
_____
_____
_____

Day 25

"Am I getting closer or farther away from my goals? What must I do to remain on track?"

It is very easy to be derailed from our goals because of the challenges and distractions we face daily. This question allows you to know what you need to do to remain on track and successfully achieve your goals.

_____
_____
_____
_____
_____
_____
_____
_____
_____

Day 26

"Do I know anybody who exudes the kind of confidence I desire?"

"How can I be more like that person?"

If you are not confident enough, you need to find someone whose confidence you can emulate and, in time, make your own.

_____
_____
_____
_____
_____
_____
_____
_____
_____

Day 27

"What steps do I need to take to conquer one of my fears?"

You need to take active measures to conquer your fears if you want to be a better person. By choosing one fear, even the most innocuous one, and conquering it, you slowly gain the courage to tackle the bigger fears.

_____
_____
_____
_____
_____
_____
_____
_____
_____

Day 28

"What are some of my favorite quotations or phrases?"

This question allows you to understand which quotes best resonate with you and what keeps you going.

_____
_____
_____
_____
_____
_____
_____
_____
_____
_____

Day 29

"Who are the individuals who make a difference in my life?"

"How do they make an impact?"

We need to take cognizance of the role important people play in our lives and how they impact our lives positively. Recognizing them will enable us to appreciate them more.

_____
_____
_____
_____
_____
_____
_____
_____

Day 30

"How frequently do I succumb to the views of others?"

It is very easy for people, including black men, to discard our opinions. Most times, unconsciously, we might be succumbing to other people's views. This is not a good sign, especially if you do it frequently. By recognizing when you're being influenced by others, you can take the necessary steps to become more grounded and confident in your own abilities and beliefs.

Day 31

"What is it about my physique that I admire the most?"

Part of accepting yourself for who you are is being able to love yourself. This question allows you to know what physical features you admire.

_____

_____

_____

_____

_____

_____

_____

_____

_____

_____

_____

Day 32

"What activities make me feel energized, satisfied, and alive?"

_____

_____

_____

_____

_____

_____

_____

_____

_____

_____

_____

Day 33

"How frequently do I have doubts about my professional or personal abilities?"

_____

_____

_____

_____

_____

_____

_____

_____

_____

_____

_____

_____

Day 34

"Is my self-confidence a result of positive self-talk (or the opposite)?"

What is the foundation of your self-confidence?

_____

_____

_____

_____

_____

_____

_____

_____

_____

Day 35

"Am I always confident regardless of the situation I find myself in?"

For some reason, our confidence level may not be high. At times, because of what we have faced in life, we do not feel confident. You need to remind yourself that you can stay confident irrespective of what life throws at you.

_____

_____

_____

_____

_____

_____

_____

_____

_____

_____

_____

_____

_____

_____

_____

_____

_____

_____

_____

_____

_____

_____

_____

_____

_____

_____

_____

_____

Day 36

"How can I fix the things in my life that make me feel uneasy?"

This question allows you to take charge of your life.

_____

_____

_____

_____

_____

_____

_____

_____

_____

_____

Day 37

"As a black woman, how do I treat people who make me happy?"

_____

_____

_____

_____

_____

_____

_____

_____

_____

_____

_____

_____

Day 38

"Who are the individuals in my life that bring me down?"

"What exactly are they doing that makes me feel this way?"

_____

_____

_____

_____

_____

_____

_____

_____

_____

_____

_____

Day 39

"What does setting boundaries mean to me?"

Setting boundaries is the one process of building courage. Boundaries help us form and sustain relationships that are critical and help us unlearn negative thought habits and myths about power dynamics.

_____

_____

_____

_____

_____

_____

_____

_____

_____

Day 40

"Do I set boundaries?"

"How do I enforce them?"

"How do people feel when I set boundaries?"

_____
_____
_____
_____
_____
_____
_____
_____
_____
_____

Day 41

"What results have boundaries given me?"

_____
_____
_____
_____
_____
_____
_____
_____
_____
_____

Day 42

"Who am I easily accessible to?"

"Who do I feel safe with?"

Being a black woman can make you doubt people. Growing up, it is possible to have had even the most trusted family member fail us. If the people we were supposed to trust constantly failed us, how is it possible to learn to trust anyone? Past trauma can make you build a strong wall even with people closest to you.

Day 43

"What can I do to surround myself with individuals who will support me?"

In many situations, we find ourselves being the only black woman in our immediate environment. Finding good people that share our struggles can be hard—because of this, having a support system or a village is very important.

_____

_____

_____

_____

_____

_____

_____

_____

_____

_____

Day 44

"Which black woman that I admire worked on their low esteem?"

"How did they do it? Am I ready to try what they did?"

_____

_____

_____

_____

_____

_____

_____

_____

_____

Day 45

"What compliments or recognition have I received from others?"

"What comments did they make?"

_____
_____
_____
_____
_____
_____
_____
_____
_____
_____
_____
_____
_____

Day 46

"Why am I important?"

_____
_____
_____
_____
_____
_____
_____
_____
_____
_____
_____

Day 47

"What makes my life, my job, and my presence so important?"

_____

_____

_____

_____

_____

_____

_____

_____

_____

_____

_____

Day 48

"What can I do today to make myself proud?"

"How can I be proud of being a black woman?"

_____

_____

_____

_____

_____

_____

_____

_____

_____

Day 49

"On what previous occasions in my life have I acted like a queen?"

_____
_____
_____
_____
_____
_____
_____
_____
_____
_____
_____
_____

Day 50

"In which previous instances did I act like a warrior?"

_____
_____
_____
_____
_____
_____
_____
_____
_____
_____
_____
_____

Day 51

"On which previous occasions have I acted like a hero?"

Being a hero in some situations can be good. But remember that you need to save yourself first.

_____

_____

_____

_____

_____

_____

_____

_____

_____

_____

_____

_____

_____

Day 52

"What do people do that makes me feel happy and excited?"

_____

_____

_____

_____

_____

_____

_____

_____

_____

_____

Day 53

"What skills do I have that I could teach others?"

_____

_____

_____

_____

_____

_____

_____

_____

_____

Day 54

"What superpower do I have?"

As a Black woman, navigating the world poses distinct obstacles that need a certain skill set, including adaptability, steadfast resolve, discipline, confidence, and so much more. To achieve success over our privileged rivals, we must be able to pivot quickly and multitask while preserving our mental health.

_____

_____

_____

_____

_____

_____

_____

_____

_____

_____

_____

Day 55

"What would I change about myself if I had the chance?"

_____

_____

_____

_____

_____

_____

_____

_____

_____

_____

_____

_____

Day 56

"What makes me an extraordinary black woman?"

_____

_____

_____

_____

_____

_____

_____

_____

_____

_____

_____

Day 57

"What adjustments can I make to improve my alone time?"

No matter how you try to be there for others, you need to make time for yourself. When you get the time, you have to make the most of it.

_____
_____
_____
_____
_____
_____
_____
_____
_____

Day 58

"What hobbies spark my interest?"

"What can I do to make the next 48 hours more enjoyable and exciting?"

_____
_____
_____
_____
_____
_____
_____
_____
_____
_____
_____

Day 59

"Which of my favorite hobbies make me happy?"

_____

_____

_____

_____

_____

_____

_____

_____

_____

_____

Day 60

"What behaviors do I need to change this year in order to increase my happiness and confidence?"

_____

_____

_____

_____

_____

_____

_____

_____

_____

Day 61

"What would it be like to do something for myself every day?"

_____

_____

_____

_____

_____

_____

_____

_____

_____

_____

_____

Day 62

"What difference would being committed to a hobby make in my life?"

_____

_____

_____

_____

_____

_____

_____

_____

_____

_____

_____

_____

Day 63

"Will my hobbies change my life positively for the next six months?"

_____

_____

_____

_____

_____

_____

_____

_____

_____

_____

Day 64

"What would it take for me to be able to love myself regardless of the trauma I have endured as a black woman?"

The trauma you have faced all your life can make you hate yourself. Self-hate can cause various things, including self-harm. You need to love yourself.

_____

_____

_____

_____

_____

_____

_____

_____

_____

_____

Day 65

"How open am I about my emotions?"

"Who do I share them with?"

Emotions are not something that most black women are encouraged to show. Changing this narrative will be good for you.

_____

_____

_____

_____

_____

_____

_____

_____

_____

_____

Day 66

"What are my strategies for dealing with tough but important conversations?"

"When I have these conversations, do I get positive results?"

_____

_____

_____

_____

_____

_____

_____

_____

_____

_____

Day 67

"What demotivates me?"

"How can I re-motivate myself?"

Remember that you only have yourself. Even if you have people constantly motivating you, you still need to prepare your mind to push you to keep going.

_____
_____
_____
_____
_____
_____
_____
_____
_____
_____

Day 68

"When was the last time I felt betrayed or wronged?"

"How did I react?"

_____
_____
_____
_____
_____
_____
_____
_____
_____
_____

Day 69

"In what ways do I stand in the way of my own happiness as a black woman?"

You might be the one hindering your happiness. So take time to think and reflect on your answer.

_____

_____

_____

_____

_____

_____

_____

_____

_____

Day 70

"When I first wake up and when I go to bed, how do I usually feel?"

Waking up or going to bed feeling tired, drowsy, or down? Do you need to figure out what is going on?

_____

_____

_____

_____

_____

_____

_____

_____

_____

_____

Day 71

"When I get into relationships, am I primarily motivated by love or by fear? What really motivates me?"

_____
_____
_____
_____
_____
_____
_____
_____
_____
_____
_____

Day 72

"Do the folks I hang out with make me feel better or worse?"

Do you need to change your circle?

_____
_____
_____
_____
_____
_____
_____
_____
_____
_____

Day 73

"How frequently do I show myself love and respect?"

You need to be deliberate about showing yourself respect and love.

_____

_____

_____

_____

_____

_____

_____

_____

_____

_____

_____

Day 74

"What is it that makes me feel limited?"

_____

_____

_____

_____

_____

_____

_____

_____

_____

_____

_____

_____

Day 75

"Is there someone I need to forgive who has wronged me in the past?"

What did the person do to hurt you? Holding on to it does not help.

_____
_____
_____
_____
_____
_____
_____
_____
_____
_____
_____

Day 76

"What have I been putting off because I am afraid of failing?"

_____
_____
_____
_____
_____
_____
_____
_____
_____
_____
_____
_____

Day 77

"Have I had any quote-worthy moments recently? What made me feel this way?"

_____
_____
_____
_____
_____
_____
_____
_____
_____

Day 78

"What makes me feel uneasy in social situations?"

"How can I prevent these things from happening?"

_____
_____
_____
_____
_____
_____
_____
_____
_____
_____
_____
_____
_____
_____

Day 79

"What are some regrets from my past and my concerns for the future?"

As a black woman, are there things and mentalities you need to let go of if you want to be a better person?

_____
_____
_____
_____
_____
_____
_____
_____
_____
_____
_____
_____
_____

Day 80

"What are some things people around me do that irritate me?"

_____
_____
_____
_____
_____
_____
_____
_____
_____
_____

Day 81

"What was the happiest moment you had in the last month?"

You need to be conscious of the little things that make you happy. Record them to have a mental replay.

_____

_____

_____

_____

_____

_____

_____

_____

_____

_____

Day 82

"What do I generally think about when I can't sleep at night?"

"Do I think about these things very often?"

_____

_____

_____

_____

_____

_____

_____

_____

_____

Day 83

"When I look in the mirror, what do I see? How do I feel?"

Do you see a confident black woman? Do you see someone who is deserving of good things?

_____
_____
_____
_____
_____
_____
_____
_____
_____
_____
_____
_____

Day 84

"In my personal interactions, what excellent attributes do I bring?"

_____
_____
_____
_____
_____
_____
_____
_____
_____

Day 85

"What duties and obligations do my colleagues entrust to me?"

Are they things you enjoy doing? Do you want to change anything?

_____

_____

_____

_____

_____

_____

_____

_____

_____

_____

_____

_____

Day 86

"What are some of the ways in which I give back to my family, organization, or community?"

_____

_____

_____

_____

_____

_____

_____

_____

_____

_____

_____

Day 87

"What activities make me happy, energetic, and satisfied?"

How often do you do them? Do you need to create time for these things?

_____

_____

_____

_____

_____

_____

_____

_____

_____

_____

_____

Day 88

"In the next five years, what skills do I wish to learn?"

How do you intend to achieve this feat?

_____

_____

_____

_____

_____

_____

_____

_____

_____

Day 89

"What are my plans for getting back on my feet following a setback?"

_____

_____

_____

_____

_____

_____

_____

_____

_____

_____

Day 90

"What risks and possibilities do I perceive in my life right now?"

_____

_____

_____

_____

_____

_____

_____

_____

_____

_____

_____

_____

Day 91

"What are some of the things I do that take up too much of my time?"

Are these things productive?

_____
_____
_____
_____
_____
_____
_____
_____
_____
_____
_____
_____
_____

Day 92

"What are some of the things I don't spend enough time doing?"

_____
_____
_____
_____
_____
_____
_____
_____
_____
_____
_____

Day 93

"What do I think I need to do for better time management?"

_____

_____

_____

_____

_____

_____

_____

_____

_____

_____

_____

Day 94

"What topic can I give a 30-minute speech impromptu?"

You need to take time to think about the answer to this question. Your answer could unlock something.

_____

_____

_____

_____

_____

_____

_____

_____

_____

_____

Day 95

"What negative traits do people think I have?"

Why do you think people feel this way about you?

_____

_____

_____

_____

_____

_____

_____

_____

_____

_____

_____

_____

Day 96

"What do family and friends frequently ask for when they come to me for assistance?"

_____

_____

_____

_____

_____

_____

_____

_____

_____

_____

_____

Day 97

"What do I generally ask for when I seek assistance from others?"

_____

_____

_____

_____

_____

_____

_____

_____

_____

_____

_____

Day 98

"What do I think about when I am alone?"

Do you have sad and depressing thoughts when you are alone? Do you need to change some thoughts you have when alone?

_____

_____

_____

_____

_____

_____

_____

_____

_____

_____

Day 99

"What are three questions I wish I knew the answers to?"

Will the answers to these questions put you in a better place or hurt you?

_____
_____
_____
_____
_____
_____
_____
_____
_____
_____
_____
_____

Day 100

"What are my greatest strengths and weaknesses?"

_____
_____
_____
_____
_____
_____
_____
_____
_____
_____
_____

Day 101

"What's one choice from the past I would alter if I could?"

_____

_____

_____

_____

_____

_____

_____

_____

_____

_____

_____

_____

_____

Day 102

"What limiting ideas do I think I have?"

_____

_____

_____

_____

_____

_____

_____

_____

_____

_____

_____

Day 103

"What do I need to say to myself right now?"

_____
_____
_____
_____
_____
_____
_____
_____
_____
_____

Day 104

"What is something I would never give up?"

_____
_____
_____
_____
_____
_____
_____
_____
_____
_____

Day 105

"What is the stupidest choice I have made?"

What steps do you need to take to not find yourself in this situation again?

_____

_____

_____

_____

_____

_____

_____

_____

_____

_____

_____

Day 106

"What is the wisest choice I have made in my life?"

_____

_____

_____

_____

_____

_____

_____

_____

_____

_____

Day 107

"What was the most beneficial thing I did for myself today?"

You need to be deliberate about self-love and self-care. Every day, you should take conscious steps to take care of yourself, no matter how small it may seem.

_____
_____
_____
_____
_____
_____
_____
_____
_____
_____
_____
_____
_____
_____

Day 108

"When was the last time I caught myself off guard?"

_____
_____
_____
_____
_____
_____
_____
_____
_____
_____
_____

Day 109

"When was the last time I learned something new?"

Just like any other gender or race, we black women have to learn new things so that we are not left behind. Even if it is a new word, try to learn it.

_____

_____

_____

_____

_____

_____

_____

_____

_____

_____

Day 110

"Who do I compare myself to constantly?"

Self-esteem issues can make us compare ourselves to others. For your own good, you need to stop.

_____

_____

_____

_____

_____

_____

_____

_____

_____

Day 111

"What was the most difficult life lesson I had to learn?"

How did it make you feel?

_____

_____

_____

_____

_____

_____

_____

_____

_____

_____

_____

Day 112

"Do I ask enough questions or rely on what I already know?"

Summon the courage to ask questions about things you don't understand, no matter how meaningless you think the question is.

_____

_____

_____

_____

_____

_____

_____

_____

_____

Day 113

"Is sobbing a show of strength or weakness?"

What is the reason for your answer?

_____

_____

_____

_____

_____

_____

_____

_____

_____

_____

_____

_____

Day 114

"How long would I keep a friend who talks to me in the same manner that I constantly speak to myself?"

_____

_____

_____

_____

_____

_____

_____

_____

_____

_____

Day 115

"Am I clinging to anything I should let go of?"

"What is the thing(s)?"

Will you feel better if you let go of it?

_____

_____

_____

_____

_____

_____

_____

_____

_____

_____

_____

Day 116

"What will be most important to me when I am 80 years old?"

_____

_____

_____

_____

_____

_____

_____

_____

_____

_____

Day 117

"When is it time to quit weighing risks and benefits?"

Do you get a sign? What is the sign?

_____

_____

_____

_____

_____

_____

_____

_____

_____

_____

Day 118

"Can I violate the law to rescue someone I care about?"

How does this make you feel?

_____

_____

_____

_____

_____

_____

_____

_____

_____

_____

_____

Day 119

"How do I show respect to myself?"

_____

_____

_____

_____

_____

_____

_____

_____

_____

_____

Day 120

"How would I conduct my life differently if I was to die at the age of 40?"

Life is very short. Do things you do not have the courage to do. Take that trip; speak to that person. You never know what will come out of it.

_____

_____

_____

_____

_____

_____

_____

_____

_____

_____

Day 121

"What advice would I offer to an infant if I could only give one piece of advice?"

_____
_____
_____
_____
_____
_____
_____
_____
_____
_____

Day 122

"Is it more important to do things right or to do the right things?"

_____
_____
_____
_____
_____
_____
_____
_____
_____
_____
_____
_____

Day 123

"What has life taught me lately?"

_____

_____

_____

_____

_____

_____

_____

_____

_____

_____

_____

Day 124

"Where do I get my ideas from?"

_____

_____

_____

_____

_____

_____

_____

_____

_____

_____

Day 125

"What kind of impression do I want to make on the whole world?"

_____

_____

_____

_____

_____

_____

_____

_____

_____

_____

Day 126

"What am I missing out on in my day-to-day rush?"

Sometimes you need to relax and pay attention to little things in your busy life.

_____

_____

_____

_____

_____

_____

_____

_____

_____

_____

Day 127

"When life gets me down, what cheers me up?"

_____
_____
_____
_____
_____
_____
_____
_____
_____
_____
_____

Day 128

"Have I ever regretted not saying or doing something?"

_____
_____
_____
_____
_____
_____
_____
_____
_____
_____
_____
_____

Day 129

"What kind of interpersonal issues do I have (with family, friends, and coworkers)?"

_____

_____

_____

_____

_____

_____

_____

_____

_____

_____

Day 130

"How do I relate with my family?"

_____

_____

_____

_____

_____

_____

_____

_____

_____

_____

_____

_____

Day 131

"What can I change about myself now that I will see results in in the next 48 hours?"

_____
_____
_____
_____
_____
_____
_____
_____
_____
_____
_____

Day 132

"Have I ever had my worst nightmare come true? What caused the incident? Was it an internal or external cause?"

_____
_____
_____
_____
_____
_____
_____
_____
_____
_____
_____

Day 133

"Who do I think about the most?"

"What impact do they have in my life?"

Day 134

"Would it help or damage me if I faced the consequences of my major decisions?"

Day 135

"If I could alter one thing if I had the opportunity to travel back in time, what would it be?"

_____
_____
_____
_____
_____
_____
_____
_____
_____
_____
_____
_____

Day 136

"Is there a distinction between innocence and ignorance?"

_____
_____
_____
_____
_____
_____
_____
_____
_____
_____
_____

Day 137

"What did my gut tell me today?"

_____

_____

_____

_____

_____

_____

_____

_____

_____

Day 138

"Is it possible to be perfect?"

How will you feel if you discover that the person you admire the most has lots of imperfections? So stop being hard on yourself girl!

_____

_____

_____

_____

_____

_____

_____

_____

_____

_____

_____

_____

Day 139

"How much control do I think I have had over the path my life has taken?"

_____

_____

_____

_____

_____

_____

_____

_____

_____

_____

Day 140

"Where would I want to travel the most, and why?"

Do you need to take some steps to make traveling a reality?

_____

_____

_____

_____

_____

_____

_____

_____

_____

_____

_____

_____

_____

Day 141

"What do I see myself doing in 10 years?"

Day 142

"What was the last act of kindness I received that I will never forget?"

Day 143

"Which of my childhood memories is the happiest?"

"What distinguishes it from the rest?"

_____

_____

_____

_____

_____

_____

_____

_____

_____

_____

Day 144

"Do I own my possessions, or do they own me?"

"What puts me in this position?"

_____

_____

_____

_____

_____

_____

_____

_____

_____

_____

Day 145

"Would I rather lose all of my past memories or be unable to create any new ones?"

Remember that memories are unique.

_____
_____
_____
_____
_____
_____
_____
_____
_____
_____

Day 146

"As a black woman, how do I deal with a powerful person who wants me to fail?"

If you are unsure of your answer, try speaking to your mentor, therapist, or someone with such experience.

_____
_____
_____
_____
_____
_____
_____
_____
_____
_____

Day 147

"What is something I can't live without?"

Is your whole existence built on this thing? What will happen if you try to get yourself away from this thing?

_____

_____

_____

_____

_____

_____

_____

_____

_____

_____

_____

Day 148

"What is one thing I haven't done yet that I really want to?"

_____

_____

_____

_____

_____

_____

_____

_____

_____

_____

_____

Day 149

"What do I have to lose if I do what I really want to do?"

_____
_____
_____
_____
_____
_____
_____
_____
_____
_____
_____

Day 150

"How would you define 'freedom'?"

_____
_____
_____
_____
_____
_____
_____
_____
_____
_____

Day 151

"What is the essential thing I can accomplish in my personal life right now?"

_____

_____

_____

_____

_____

_____

_____

_____

_____

_____

_____

Day 152

"Who would I ask if I could only pose one question to someone I admire, living or dead?"

_____

_____

_____

_____

_____

_____

_____

_____

_____

_____

_____

Day 153

"What is your most important objective over the next six months?"

_____

_____

_____

_____

_____

_____

_____

_____

_____

_____

_____

Day 154

"Would I ever put my own life on the line to help someone else? Will it be a random person or not?"

_____

_____

_____

_____

_____

_____

_____

_____

_____

_____

Day 155

"Am I content with who I am?"

What do you think fuels this feeling?

_____

_____

_____

_____

_____

_____

_____

_____

_____

_____

Day 156

"If my life was a movie, what would it look like?"

Will it be sad, boring, interesting, fun, or depressing?

_____

_____

_____

_____

_____

_____

_____

_____

_____

_____

Day 157

"What time of day do I feel the most like myself?"

_____

_____

_____

_____

_____

_____

_____

_____

_____

_____

_____

Day 158

"Do I ever wonder, 'What's in it for me?' when I assist someone?"

_____

_____

_____

_____

_____

_____

_____

_____

_____

_____

_____

Day 159

"Would I want to know the precise day and hour I am going to die if someone could tell me?"

_____

_____

_____

_____

_____

_____

_____

_____

_____

_____

_____

_____

Day 160

"Which day of my life would I choose to experience again?"

_____

_____

_____

_____

_____

_____

_____

_____

_____

_____

_____

Day 161

"What would I do if I had the chance to experience the next 24 hours, delete everything and start over?"

_____

_____

_____

_____

_____

_____

_____

_____

_____

Day 162

"When I discover the truth or true meanings and way of things, will I accept it?"

When we are used to a specific way of doing things and we gain new knowledge, it can be hard to welcome and accept change. We learn every day. We should be open to unlearning, learning, and relearning.

_____

_____

_____

_____

_____

_____

_____

_____

_____

_____

_____

Day 163

"What comes to mind when *I* think of the word 'home'?"

Is it a safe space? Is it toxic?

_____
_____
_____
_____
_____
_____
_____
_____
_____
_____
_____

Day 164

"What's the difference between accepting things as they are and settling?"

_____
_____
_____
_____
_____
_____
_____
_____
_____
_____
_____

Day 165

"Do I have any friends I trust my life with?"

Do you believe that they feel the same way about you? What is the reason for your answer?

_____
_____
_____
_____
_____
_____
_____
_____
_____
_____
_____
_____

Day 166

"Who is standing in the way of my happiness?"

_____
_____
_____
_____
_____
_____
_____
_____
_____
_____
_____
_____

Day 167

"What factors contribute to a person's attractiveness?"

_____
_____
_____
_____
_____
_____
_____
_____
_____
_____
_____
_____

Day 168

"Is there a moment when it's better to give up?"

_____
_____
_____
_____
_____
_____
_____
_____
_____
_____
_____

Day 169

"What do I take pride in?"

_____

_____

_____

_____

_____

_____

_____

_____

_____

_____

_____

Day 170

"When was the last time I worked hard and enjoyed every second of it?"

_____

_____

_____

_____

_____

_____

_____

_____

_____

_____

_____

Day 171

"When does silence speak louder than words?"

_____
_____
_____
_____
_____
_____
_____
_____
_____
_____
_____
_____

Day 172

"What do I do with most of my leisure time?"

_____
_____
_____
_____
_____
_____
_____
_____
_____
_____
_____
_____

Day 173

"When I think about success, what (or who) comes to mind?"

_____

_____

_____

_____

_____

_____

_____

_____

_____

_____

_____

Day 174

"When I was a kid, what did I want to be when I grew up?"

_____

_____

_____

_____

_____

_____

_____

_____

_____

_____

_____

Day 175

"In five years, how will today's events be remembered?"

_____
_____
_____
_____
_____
_____
_____
_____
_____
_____
_____

Day 176

"Do I believe to see or see to believe?"

_____
_____
_____
_____
_____
_____
_____
_____
_____
_____

Day 177

"When does love become a flaw?"

What recent love have you seen that changed your mindset?

_____

_____

_____

_____

_____

_____

_____

_____

_____

_____

_____

Day 178

"What has been the most horrifying experience I have had thus far in my life?"

_____

_____

_____

_____

_____

_____

_____

_____

_____

_____

_____

Day 179

"How am I currently pursuing my goals?"

_____

_____

_____

_____

_____

_____

_____

_____

_____

_____

_____

Day 180

"What have I accomplished in the previous year that I am proud of?"

_____

_____

_____

_____

_____

_____

_____

_____

_____

_____

_____

Day 181

"What have I learned over the years that have positively transformed the way I live my life?"

_____

_____

_____

_____

_____

_____

_____

_____

_____

_____

_____

_____

Day 182

"What is my most memorable experience over the last three years?"

_____

_____

_____

_____

_____

_____

_____

_____

_____

_____

_____

Day 183

"What are the most important aspects of a happy life?"

_____

_____

_____

_____

_____

_____

_____

_____

_____

_____

_____

Day 184

"What can I do right now with the resources I have to get closer to my goal?"

_____

_____

_____

_____

_____

_____

_____

_____

Day 185

"What is the finest thing I have ever received from someone?"

_____

_____

_____

_____

_____

_____

_____

_____

_____

_____

Day 186

"When I gaze into the future, what do I see?"

_____

_____

_____

_____

_____

_____

_____

_____

_____

_____

_____

Day 187

"What simple pleasures do I like the most?"

_____
_____
_____
_____
_____
_____
_____
_____
_____
_____

Day 188

"What do I do to make a conscious effort to impress others?"

_____
_____
_____
_____
_____
_____
_____
_____
_____
_____
_____

Day 189

"What is the most intense peer pressure I have ever experienced?"

_____

_____

_____

_____

_____

_____

_____

_____

_____

_____

Day 190

"What's the greatest lie I used to believe as a black woman? What made me realize it was a lie?"

_____

_____

_____

_____

_____

_____

_____

_____

_____

_____

_____

Day 191

"What have I done in my life that has caused someone else harm?"

_____
_____
_____
_____
_____
_____
_____
_____
_____
_____
_____

Day 192

"What is the most enjoyable aspect of becoming older?"

_____
_____
_____
_____
_____
_____
_____
_____
_____
_____
_____
_____

Day 193

"Am I content with my current situation? Why or why not?"

_____

_____

_____

_____

_____

_____

_____

_____

_____

_____

Day 194

"What is the most significant roadblock I am currently facing?"

_____

_____

_____

_____

_____

_____

_____

_____

_____

_____

_____

Day 195

"What do I pretend to comprehend when I really don't?"

_____

_____

_____

_____

_____

_____

_____

_____

_____

_____

_____

Day 196

"What's something you have discovered about yourself recently?"

_____

_____

_____

_____

_____

_____

_____

_____

_____

_____

_____

Day 197

"What was the most pivotal event in my life during the last 12 months?"

_____
_____
_____
_____
_____
_____
_____
_____
_____
_____
_____
_____

Day 198

"When was the last time my initial impression of someone was incorrect?"

_____
_____
_____
_____
_____
_____
_____
_____
_____
_____
_____
_____

Day 199

"How many hours do I spend online each week?"

_____

_____

_____

_____

_____

_____

_____

_____

_____

_____

_____

Day 200

"'What is the most important characteristic of a good leader?"

_____

_____

_____

_____

_____

_____

_____

_____

_____

_____

Day 201

"What negative habits would I want to get rid of?"

_____

_____

_____

_____

_____

_____

_____

_____

_____

Day 202

"What is my favorite spot in the world?"

Do you believe if you put yourself out there, go out more, or travel more, your answer will change?

_____

_____

_____

_____

_____

_____

_____

_____

_____

_____

_____

_____

Day 203

"What's the status of my regrets in my life?"

_____

_____

_____

_____

_____

_____

_____

_____

_____

_____

Day 204

"What, if anything, would I alter in my life right now if I had the chance?"

_____

_____

_____

_____

_____

_____

_____

_____

_____

_____

_____

Day 205

"Have I forgiven my parents/family members for their mistakes?"

Forgiving is very important in healing. Forgiving others is for your own good, not theirs.

_____

_____

_____

_____

_____

_____

_____

_____

_____

_____

_____

_____

Day 206

"Have I embraced my childhood for what it was?"

_____

_____

_____

_____

_____

_____

_____

_____

_____

Day 207

"Am I content with who I am as a person?"

_____

_____

_____

_____

_____

_____

_____

_____

_____

_____

_____

Day 208

"Is the tiny kid I once was proud of who I am now?"

Will your old self be proud of who you are now? What will your old self be proud of?
What do you want your old self to be proud of?

_____

_____

_____

_____

_____

_____

_____

_____

_____

_____

_____

_____

Day 209

"In every aspect of my life, am I living as healthily as possible?"

In your self-discovery journey, do not forget to stay healthy. Do you need to change your diet or lifestyle?

_____

_____

_____

_____

_____

_____

_____

_____

_____

_____

_____

_____

_____

Day 210

"Have I begun to see my parents as individuals with ambitions, dreams, and flaws?"

_____

_____

_____

_____

_____

_____

_____

_____

_____

_____

Day 211

"Do I understand how to live in the moment?"

_____

_____

_____

_____

_____

_____

_____

_____

_____

_____

_____

_____

Day 212

"Do I recognize my flaws?"

"What are these flaws?"

_____

_____

_____

_____

_____

_____

_____

_____

_____

_____

_____

Day 213

"Do I recognize my finest qualities?"

_____
_____
_____
_____
_____
_____
_____
_____
_____

Day 214

"Do I have at least one person in my life who will always tell me the truth about myself, no matter how painful it is?"

_____
_____
_____
_____
_____
_____
_____
_____
_____
_____
_____
_____

Day 215

"Do I have any idea how to make peace with my past?"

_____
_____
_____
_____
_____
_____
_____
_____
_____
_____
_____

Day 216

"Do I have a life that I am happy with?"

_____
_____
_____
_____
_____
_____
_____
_____
_____
_____
_____
_____

Day 217

"Do I have a group of individuals that are emotionally and psychologically supportive of me?"

_____

_____

_____

_____

_____

_____

_____

_____

_____

Day 218

"Are my ties with my family fulfilling to me?"

Just because they are family doesn't mean that they will make you happy. If they are toxic to your general wellbeing, what do you need to do to make sure they do not interrupt your self-discovery journey?

_____

_____

_____

_____

_____

_____

_____

_____

_____

_____

Day 219

"Outside of societal expectations for what a woman should look like, am I content with the body I have?"

_____

_____

_____

_____

_____

_____

_____

_____

_____

_____

Day 220

"What is beauty to me?"

_____

_____

_____

_____

_____

_____

_____

_____

_____

_____

_____

_____

Day 221

"Is it possible for me to identify my core beliefs?"

_____

_____

_____

_____

_____

_____

_____

_____

_____

_____

_____

Day 222

"Is it possible for me to feel confident in my beliefs even when others disagree with me?"

_____

_____

_____

_____

_____

_____

_____

_____

_____

_____

_____

Day 223

"Does my behavior reflect my personal beliefs and values?"

When there is a disconnect between your beliefs and values, you will be living an inconsistent life. Right now, write down the bad habits you have. Then write down your most important values and beliefs. Afterward, begin to root out the inconsistencies.

_____

_____

_____

_____

_____

_____

_____

_____

_____

_____

_____

_____

_____

_____

_____

_____

_____

_____

_____

_____

_____

_____

_____

_____

_____

_____

_____

Day 224

"Do I spend time with folks who have opinions that are diametrically opposed to my own?"

_____

_____

_____

_____

_____

_____

_____

_____

_____

_____

_____

_____

Day 225

"Do the individuals I spend time with like and respect me?"

_____

_____

_____

_____

_____

_____

_____

_____

_____

_____

Day 226

"Do I understand what it's like to be alone?"

_____
_____
_____
_____
_____
_____
_____
_____
_____
_____
_____
_____

Day 227

"No matter what my relationship situation is, am I content with myself?"

_____
_____
_____
_____
_____
_____
_____
_____
_____
_____
_____

Day 228

"Do I offer enough of myself and my possessions to the people I care about?"

_____

_____

_____

_____

_____

_____

_____

_____

_____

_____

Day 229

"Do I want to change to try something new or to get away from issues that I don't want to deal with?"

_____

_____

_____

_____

_____

_____

_____

_____

_____

_____

_____

_____

_____

Day 230

"Is my living condition and space exactly what I want?"

"Do I need to make changes?"

_____
_____
_____
_____
_____
_____
_____
_____
_____
_____

Day 231

"Is this the correct location or town for my life right now?"

Being in the wrong place or location can hinder growth in any area of your life.

_____
_____
_____
_____
_____
_____
_____
_____
_____

Day 232

"Is the way I spend my money a reflection of who I am or aspire to be?"

_____

_____

_____

_____

_____

_____

_____

_____

_____

Day 233

"Is my employment satisfying to me?"

You need to know if you're in a toxic work environment or not. Do you have colleagues or bosses that make you feel good or worthless? Assess the general conditions of your workplace.

_____

_____

_____

_____

_____

_____

_____

_____

_____

_____

_____

Day 234

"Is what I'm doing right now a job or a career?"

Does your current job put you on the right track to achieving your goals?

_____

_____

_____

_____

_____

_____

_____

_____

_____

_____

_____

_____

_____

_____

Day 235

"Am I developing the abilities and forming the connections that I require?"

_____

_____

_____

_____

_____

_____

_____

_____

_____

_____

_____

Day 236

"Do I know how to build a mutually beneficial network?"

_____
_____
_____
_____
_____
_____
_____
_____
_____
_____

Day 237

"What is my favorite personal non-physical characteristic?"

_____
_____
_____
_____
_____
_____
_____
_____
_____
_____

Day 238

"What social customs would I want to see vanish?"

_____

_____

_____

_____

_____

_____

_____

_____

_____

_____

_____

Day 239

"What is one thing I've learned that the majority of people aren't aware of?"

_____

_____

_____

_____

_____

_____

_____

_____

_____

_____

_____

Day 240

"What is the role of love and affection in my life?"

_____
_____
_____
_____
_____
_____
_____
_____
_____
_____
_____
_____

Day 241

"Do I have any self-confidence issues?"

_____
_____
_____
_____
_____
_____
_____
_____
_____
_____
_____
_____

Day 242

"What is one memory from my childhood that I hope I never forget?

_____

_____

_____

_____

_____

_____

_____

_____

_____

_____

_____

_____

Day 243

"What qualities do I value in a friendship?"

_____

_____

_____

_____

_____

_____

_____

_____

_____

_____

_____

Day 244

"What is/was my longest-lasting friendship, and how did I keep it going for so long?"

_____

_____

_____

_____

_____

_____

_____

_____

_____

_____

_____

Day 245

"Do I believe I can have more than one best friend?"

_____

_____

_____

_____

_____

_____

_____

_____

_____

_____

_____

Day 246

"Do I regard my parents as the best?"

_____

_____

_____

_____

_____

_____

_____

_____

_____

_____

_____

Day 247

"Do I believe that people of opposing genders can have a friendship without falling in love?"

_____

_____

_____

_____

_____

_____

_____

_____

_____

_____

Day 248

"What is an unforgivable act to me?"

_____

_____

_____

_____

_____

_____

_____

_____

_____

_____

_____

Day 249

"What recommendations would I provide to those who have long-distance friendships?"

_____

_____

_____

_____

_____

_____

_____

_____

_____

_____

_____

Day 250

"Do long-distance relationships work?"

Have you ever been in any long-distance relationship? If you could do something different about your last relationship, what would it be?

_____

_____

_____

_____

_____

_____

_____

_____

_____

Day 251

"Do I believe it's preferable to invest or save money?"

Your thoughts about what to do with your money is important. So what do you do with any spare money and income?

_____

_____

_____

_____

_____

_____

_____

_____

_____

Day 252

"What qualities do I search for in a partner?"

_____

_____

_____

_____

_____

_____

_____

_____

_____

_____

Day 253

"What is the most crucial aspect of a relationship?" (For example, trust, respect, and so on.)

_____

_____

_____

_____

_____

_____

_____

_____

_____

_____

_____

_____

Day 254

"How frequently should a couple fight in order to keep their relationship healthy?"

_____

_____

_____

_____

_____

_____

_____

_____

_____

_____

_____

Day 255

"How do I face life's challenges?"

_____

_____

_____

_____

_____

_____

_____

_____

_____

_____

_____

Day 256

"Do I like to attempt new things in order to impress others?"

_____
_____
_____
_____
_____
_____
_____
_____
_____
_____
_____

Day 257

"Would I put in more effort or seek assistance if my task became too much?"

_____
_____
_____
_____
_____
_____
_____
_____
_____
_____
_____

Day 258

"What would I alter about myself if I had the chance? Why?"

_____

_____

_____

_____

_____

_____

_____

_____

_____

_____

_____

_____

Day 259

"What can I do to help myself feel more secure?"

_____

_____

_____

_____

_____

_____

_____

_____

_____

_____

Day 260

"Do I have a secure location to escape from things and pressures in my life?"

What's the point of having one? Is it possible to face what you think you should run from?

_____

_____

_____

_____

_____

_____

_____

_____

_____

_____

_____

_____

_____

_____

Day 261

"What do I do when I am worried?"

_____

_____

_____

_____

_____

_____

_____

_____

_____

Day 262

"What is my proudest accomplishment?"

Your answer can be based on any area of your life.

_____
_____
_____
_____
_____
_____
_____
_____
_____
_____
_____
_____
_____
_____

Day 263

"Has anything impacted my perspective on life?"

_____
_____
_____
_____
_____
_____
_____
_____
_____

Day 264

"Do I consider myself to be a good decision-maker?"

"What can I do to improve?"

_____

_____

_____

_____

_____

_____

_____

_____

_____

_____

_____

_____

Day 265

"What is the most significant item in my life?"

_____

_____

_____

_____

_____

_____

_____

_____

_____

_____

_____

Day 266

"Am I focused?"

"What can I do to improve?"

_____

_____

_____

_____

_____

_____

_____

_____

_____

_____

_____

_____

_____

Day 267

"How do I react when angry?"

_____

_____

_____

_____

_____

_____

_____

_____

_____

_____

Day 268

"How honest am I in my everyday life?"

_____

_____

_____

_____

_____

_____

_____

_____

_____

_____

_____

_____

Day 269

"What is my fear-management strategy?"

_____

_____

_____

_____

_____

_____

_____

_____

_____

_____

_____

_____

Day 270

"How frequently do I let my creative side shine?"

_____

_____

_____

_____

_____

_____

_____

_____

_____

_____

_____

_____

Day 271

"What irritates or disturbs me the most?"

_____

_____

_____

_____

_____

_____

_____

_____

_____

_____

_____

_____

Day 272

"How good am I at communicating?"

_____

_____

_____

_____

_____

_____

_____

_____

_____

_____

_____

Day 273

"What is my opinion of my work ethic? Is there room for improvement?"

_____

_____

_____

_____

_____

_____

_____

_____

_____

_____

_____

_____

Day 274

"What makes life worthwhile?"

_____

_____

_____

_____

_____

_____

_____

_____

_____

_____

_____

Day 275

"How would I rate my capacity to endure and persist on a scale of 1-10?"

_____

_____

_____

_____

_____

_____

_____

_____

_____

_____

Day 276

"Am I a quitter?"

"How can I be better?"

_____

_____

_____

_____

_____

_____

_____

_____

_____

_____

Day 277

"Is it easy for me to admit my mistakes?"

Give reasons for your answer.

_____

_____

_____

_____

_____

_____

_____

_____

_____

_____

_____

Day 278

"What do I believe I should spend more time on in my life?"

"What am I most thankful for?"

_____
_____
_____
_____
_____
_____
_____
_____
_____
_____
_____
_____
_____

Day 279

"What do I really want?"

_____
_____
_____
_____
_____
_____
_____
_____
_____
_____

Day 280

"Have I discovered a balancing ritual?"

Rituals help us build routines by giving our days and lives shape and context. If you already have one, how well do you adhere to it? Be honest with yourself. If you are not following it strictly, work on it. If you do not have one, it may be time to create one.

_____

_____

_____

_____

_____

_____

_____

_____

_____

_____

_____

_____

_____

_____

_____

_____

_____

_____

_____

_____

_____

_____

_____

_____

Day 281

"What makes me happy about myself?"

_____

_____

_____

_____

_____

_____

_____

_____

_____

_____

_____

Day 282

"What makes me feel horrible about myself or guilty?"

_____

_____

_____

_____

_____

_____

_____

_____

_____

_____

Day 283

"When do I get a sense of my true self?"

_____

_____

_____

_____

_____

_____

_____

_____

_____

_____

_____

_____

Day 284

"What causes me to get enraged?"

_____

_____

_____

_____

_____

_____

_____

_____

_____

_____

_____

Day 285

"How do I handle my rage?"

_____

_____

_____

_____

_____

_____

_____

_____

_____

_____

_____

Day 286

"What makes me happy when I am down?"

_____

_____

_____

_____

_____

_____

_____

_____

_____

_____

Day 287

"How well do I adjust to life's changes?"

_____
_____
_____
_____
_____
_____
_____
_____
_____
_____
_____

Day 288

"What is my go-to method for coping with tense situations?"

_____
_____
_____
_____
_____
_____
_____
_____
_____
_____
_____
_____

Day 289

"How do I maintain my composure in the face of adversity?"

_____

_____

_____

_____

_____

_____

_____

_____

_____

_____

_____

Day 290

"Do I have a well-balanced mindset? What can I do to improve?"

_____

_____

_____

_____

_____

_____

_____

_____

_____

_____

_____

Day 291

"Do I find myself envious of others? Why?"

_____

_____

_____

_____

_____

_____

_____

_____

_____

_____

Day 292

"What quickly irritates me? Why?"

_____

_____

_____

_____

_____

_____

_____

_____

_____

Day 293

"Do I ever feel bad about situations that are beyond my control?"

Day 294

"Did I have a good chuckle or grin today? What made me do that?"

Day 295

"Do my feelings have an impact on my actions? Is the outcome favorable or unfavorable?"

_____
_____
_____
_____
_____
_____
_____
_____
_____
_____

Day 296

"Do I get mood swings?"

"What are my strategies for dealing with them?"

_____
_____
_____
_____
_____
_____
_____
_____
_____
_____
_____
_____

Day 297

"Do I find it easy to express my feelings?"

_____

_____

_____

_____

_____

_____

_____

_____

_____

_____

_____

Day 298

"Do I find myself being dissatisfied with my life on a regular basis?"

"What are my plans for dealing with it?"

_____

_____

_____

_____

_____

_____

_____

_____

_____

_____

Day 299

"Do I have any regrets in my life?"

"What are my plans for dealing with it?"

_____

_____

_____

_____

_____

_____

_____

_____

_____

Day 300

"Do I get worried and tense all the time?"

"What is the reason behind this?"

_____

_____

_____

_____

_____

_____

_____

_____

_____

_____

_____

Day 301

"Do I consider myself to be a brave person? Why?"

_____

_____

_____

_____

_____

_____

_____

_____

_____

_____

_____

Day 302

"Which of my emotions would I want to be free of? Why?"

_____

_____

_____

_____

_____

_____

_____

_____

_____

_____

_____

Day 303

"Have I ever felt in command and powerful?"

Write instances of when this happened. How did you feel when it happened?

_____
_____
_____
_____
_____
_____
_____
_____
_____
_____
_____
_____

Day 304

"How do I cope with psychological trauma?"

_____
_____
_____
_____
_____
_____
_____
_____
_____
_____

Day 305

"Can I derive enjoyment from the smallest of things?"

Day 306

"Which of my feelings do I find the most pleasurable?"

Day 307

"Have I ever experienced numbness? What was the cause for it?"

_____

_____

_____

_____

_____

_____

_____

_____

_____

_____

_____

Day 308

"Have I ever had the sensation of being completely free?" Give specifics.

_____

_____

_____

_____

_____

_____

_____

_____

_____

_____

_____

Day 309

"Do I consider myself to be a positive person?"

_____
_____
_____
_____
_____
_____
_____
_____
_____
_____
_____

Day 310

"What effect does ambiguity have on me?"

What are your plans for dealing with it?

_____
_____
_____
_____
_____
_____
_____
_____
_____
_____
_____
_____

Day 311

"What is my greatest life regret?"

_____

_____

_____

_____

_____

_____

_____

_____

_____

_____

_____

Day 312

"What would I say to someone I have previously wronged?"

_____

_____

_____

_____

_____

_____

_____

_____

_____

_____

_____

_____

Day 313

"What should I say to someone who has previously harmed me?"

_____

_____

_____

_____

_____

_____

_____

_____

_____

_____

_____

Day 314

"What makes me the most dissatisfied?"

_____

_____

_____

_____

_____

_____

_____

_____

_____

_____

_____

Day 315

"What makes me feel the most respected and appreciated?"

_____

_____

_____

_____

_____

_____

_____

_____

_____

_____

_____

_____

Day 316

"What was the most enjoyable period of my life? Why?"

_____

_____

_____

_____

_____

_____

_____

_____

_____

_____

_____

_____

Day 317

"What is one thing I have always wanted to accomplish but aren't sure whether I can?"

_____

_____

_____

_____

_____

_____

_____

_____

_____

_____

_____

_____

Day 318

"What is one thing I believe I can only achieve with the help of others?"

_____

_____

_____

_____

_____

_____

_____

_____

_____

Day 319

"What is one item I have been putting off for a long time?"

_____
_____
_____
_____
_____
_____
_____
_____
_____
_____
_____
_____

Day 320

"What is the one thing about the future that excites me?"

_____
_____
_____
_____
_____
_____
_____
_____
_____
_____
_____
_____

Day 321

"What is the perfect job for me?"

_____

_____

_____

_____

_____

_____

_____

_____

_____

_____

_____

_____

Day 322

"What are some ways I feel I might improve my self-care?"

_____

_____

_____

_____

_____

_____

_____

_____

_____

_____

Day 323

"What tasks do I constantly have on my to-do list that I keep procrastinating?"

Why do you keep procrastinating? How can you stop?

_____
_____
_____
_____
_____
_____
_____
_____
_____
_____
_____
_____
_____

Day 324

"What part of my future do I dread the most?"

_____
_____
_____
_____
_____
_____
_____
_____
_____
_____
_____
_____

Day 325

"What is the one characteristic in others that I can't stand?"

_____
_____
_____
_____
_____
_____
_____
_____
_____
_____
_____
_____

Day 326

"What is the one attribute in others that I appreciate the most?"

_____
_____
_____
_____
_____
_____
_____
_____
_____
_____
_____

Day 327

"What does it mean to love?"

_____

_____

_____

_____

_____

_____

_____

_____

_____

_____

_____

_____

Day 328

"Who is the one person I am certain will always have my back?"

_____

_____

_____

_____

_____

_____

_____

_____

_____

_____

_____

_____

Day 329

"How would I presently communicate with someone I previously mistreated?"

_____
_____
_____
_____
_____
_____
_____
_____
_____
_____

Day 330

"What qualities do I want in a best friend?"

"Do I possess such characteristics?"

_____
_____
_____
_____
_____
_____
_____
_____
_____
_____

Day 331

"How do I express my love for someone?"

_____
_____
_____
_____
_____
_____
_____
_____
_____
_____
_____

Day 332

"How attentive am I to others?"

_____
_____
_____
_____
_____
_____
_____
_____
_____
_____
_____

Day 333

"Who is my go-to person in case of an emergency? Why?"

_____
_____
_____
_____
_____
_____
_____
_____
_____
_____
_____

Day 334

"What do I want others to say about me?"

_____
_____
_____
_____
_____
_____
_____
_____
_____
_____
_____

Day 335

"Who are the individuals in my life who mean the most to me?"

_____
_____
_____
_____
_____
_____
_____
_____
_____
_____
_____

Day 336

"Who do I adore the most?"

_____
_____
_____
_____
_____
_____
_____
_____
_____
_____
_____

Day 337

"What characteristics would I want to see in a friend?"

_____
_____
_____
_____
_____
_____
_____
_____
_____
_____
_____

Day 338

"Do I desire to rekindle a relationship with someone from my past? Why?"

_____
_____
_____
_____
_____
_____
_____
_____
_____
_____
_____

Day 339

"Who do I have the greatest faith in? Why?"

_____
_____
_____
_____
_____
_____
_____
_____
_____
_____
_____

Day 340

"Is it possible for another person to make or ruin my life?"

_____
_____
_____
_____
_____
_____
_____
_____
_____
_____
_____

Day 341

"Who is the one person who has improved my life even at their own expense?"

_____
_____
_____
_____
_____
_____
_____
_____
_____
_____
_____
_____

Day 342

"Do I lend a hand to those I care about?"

_____
_____
_____
_____
_____
_____
_____
_____
_____
_____

Day 343

"When was the last time I felt the need for a real friend? Why?"

_____
_____
_____
_____
_____
_____
_____
_____
_____
_____

Day 344

"Who is my closest companion?"

"Are we a lot alike?"

_____
_____
_____
_____
_____
_____
_____
_____
_____
_____
_____

Day 345

"What are the components that make a friendship successful?"

_____
_____
_____
_____
_____
_____
_____
_____
_____
_____
_____

Day 346

"Do I express gratitude to others? How?"

_____
_____
_____
_____
_____
_____
_____
_____
_____
_____
_____

Day 347

"Do I have a plan for dealing with toxic people?"

"How do I handle toxic people even if they are black like me?"

_____

_____

_____

_____

_____

_____

_____

_____

_____

_____

_____

_____

Day 348

"How can I get along with individuals who have opposing views?"

_____

_____

_____

_____

_____

_____

_____

_____

_____

_____

Day 349

"Do I like to hang out with many people or a small group of people?"

_____
_____
_____
_____
_____
_____
_____
_____
_____
_____
_____

Day 350

"How frequently do people misunderstand me?"

"What are my plans for dealing with it?"

_____
_____
_____
_____
_____
_____
_____
_____
_____
_____
_____

Day 351

"Have I ever been through a heartbreak?"

"How did I handle it?"

_____
_____
_____
_____
_____
_____
_____
_____
_____
_____
_____

Day 352

"What is my approach to dealing with conflict?'

_____
_____
_____
_____
_____
_____
_____
_____
_____
_____

Day 353

"Do my loved ones support me in all I do?"

Do their opinions matter to you? If they do not support you, will it affect you?

_____
_____
_____
_____
_____
_____
_____
_____
_____
_____
_____
_____
_____
_____
_____
_____

Day 354

"Do I feel at ease meeting new people?"

_____
_____
_____
_____
_____
_____
_____
_____
_____
_____

Day 355

"Do I worry about what other people think of me? Why?"

_____
_____
_____
_____
_____
_____
_____
_____
_____
_____
_____
_____

Day 356

"Is it easy for me to accept folks for who they are?"

_____
_____
_____
_____
_____
_____
_____
_____
_____
_____
_____
_____

Day 357

"What are some of the behaviors and activities that make me feel good?"

_____
_____
_____
_____
_____
_____
_____
_____
_____
_____

Day 358

"Do I get enough sleep?"

"What can I do to get enough sleep or maintain a healthy sleeping schedule?"

_____
_____
_____
_____
_____
_____
_____
_____
_____

Day 359

"Do I feel energized enough today?"

What is the reason for your answer?

_____
_____
_____
_____
_____
_____
_____
_____
_____
_____

Day 360

"Am I at ease when I move my body?"

"Do I easily feel tired?"

_____
_____
_____
_____
_____
_____
_____
_____
_____
_____

Day 361

"Do I feel better when I exercise?"

_____

_____

_____

_____

_____

_____

_____

_____

_____

_____

_____

Day 362

"Am I scared of dying? Why?"

_____

_____

_____

_____

_____

_____

_____

_____

_____

_____

Day 363

"How do I deal with stress?"

_____

_____

_____

_____

_____

_____

_____

_____

_____

_____

Day 364

"Do I recognize when my body needs rest?"

"How does my body tell me to rest?"

"Do I pay heed to my body?"

_____

_____

_____

_____

_____

_____

_____

_____

_____

_____

_____

Day 365

"Is time devoted to self-care a waste?"

"Will I take out time from my schedule for self-care?"

Conclusion

Thank you for taking out time for yourself. With this book, you have asked and answered 365 questions tailored to knowing yourself better. I hope that it was a beneficial, exciting, and fulfilling experience that allowed you to gain clarity about who you are.

As you have discovered your true identity and answered profound self-discovery questions, you will continue to see the richness of your talents, purpose, and beliefs.

Even after dedicating a year to this journey, I encourage you to return to this book consistently.

Best wishes

Layla

Thank you

"Happiness springs from doing good and helping others."
— Plato

Those who help others without any expectations in return experience more fulfillment, have higher levels of success, and live longer.

I want to create the opportunity for you to do this during this reading experience. For this, I have a very simple question... If it didn't cost you money, would you help someone you've never met before, even if you never got credit for it? If so, I want to ask for a favor on behalf of someone you do not know and likely never will. They are just like you and me, or perhaps how you were a few years ago…Less experienced, filled with the desire to help the world, seeking good information but not sure where to look…this is where you can help. The only way for us at Dreamlifepress to accomplish our mission of helping people on their spiritual growth journey is to first, reach them. And most people do judge a book by its reviews. So, if you have found this book helpful, would you please take a quick moment right now to leave an honest review of the book? It will cost you nothing and less than 60 seconds. Your review will help a stranger find this book and benefit from it.

One more person finds peace and happiness…one more person may find their passion in life…one more person experience a transformation that otherwise would never have happened…To make that come true, all you have to do is to leave a review. If you're on audible, click on the three dots in the top right of your screen, rate and review. If you're reading on a e-reader or kindle, just scroll to the bottom of the book, then swipe up and it will ask for a review. If this doesn't work, you can go to the book page on amazon or wherever store you purchased this from and leave a review from that page.